HOLY WATER

AND ITS SIGNIFICANCE FOR CATHOLICS

HOLY WATER

AND ITS SIGNIFICANCE FOR CATHOLICS

FROM THE GERMAN
OF
REV. HENRY THEILER, S.O.CIST.

BY
REV. J. F. LANG

WITH A FEW SCRIPTURAL AND HISTORICAL INSERTIONS BY THE TRANSLATOR

GYAN

ISBN : 978-81-212-9006-7(HB)

First Published in 1909
Indian Reprint in 2017

Published by

GYAN

Gyan Publishing House
5, Ansari Road
Daryaganj, New Delhi-110002
E-mail: books@gyanbooks.com
Website: www.gyanbooks.com
Ph.: +91-9212142040

Episcopal Imprimatur.

We cheerfully grant the episcopal imprimatur for this booklet because it correctly presents the teaching of the Church concerning sacramentals, specifically that of Holy Water, and it likewise encourages in popular form, and from practical viewpoints to the faithful, the wholesome use of Holy Water.

Ratisbon, 28 March, 1906.

The Episcopal Ordinary,

Dr. Fr. Xav. Leitner,
Vicar-General.

AUTHOR'S FOREWORD

THE Catholic Church, the kingdom of Christ on Earth, is above all a kingdom of grace and of blessing, and the great seven-branched stream of the Holy Sacraments fruitfully permeates it, and from its waters the faithful draw grace upon grace. From one end to the other of this realm are erected the altars upon which the unbloody sacrifice of the New Testament is offered, and from them flow the streams of grace over the entire earth. Not content with these favors, holy sacramentals meander as so many rivulets of grace in holy Church, to refresh and strengthen them that draw therefrom. Of one of these sacramentals we give a short description in this booklet, — holy water. May the Heavenly Father bless this work, and by it, for His honor, achieve much good for the salvation of souls.

ABBEY MARIENSTATT,
Feast of St. Andrew, 1905.

CHAPTER I

The Significancy of Water in the Realm of Nature and of Grace

On the first page of Holy Writ we read that "the Spirit of God moved over the waters." (Gen. i. 2.) Why moved the spirit of God over the waters? The writings of the Holy Doctors make reply: To bless them, that they may become adaptable to their task in the work of creation. The holy apostle Peter thus briefly attests these tasks of the waters: "For this they (deceitful scoffers) are wilfully ignorant of, that the heavens were before, and the earth out of water, and through water, consisting by the word of God." (2 Peter iii. 5.)

And, too, after Creation, water has an important function to perform in the realm of nature, and be it said, likewise in the realm of grace. Reflect for a moment how in nature every living creature requires water, and how our springs and streams, carrying their blessings, spread over the land. They are to the soil what the circulation of the blood is to the human body. As the blood circulates from the heart throughout the body and returns, so rise the waters from the lakes, fructify the thirsty soil by refreshing rains, and return to the lakes and oceans.

And as water plays its important part in nature's kingdom, so too it does in the province of grace as the blessed and holy water.

The old Romans made use of a water which they held sacred. We are told by Ovid, Virgil, and Cicero, of a sacred water, with which the people, the homes, and the fields were sprinkled, that by this sprinkling plagues might be warded off, and sin stains wiped away. The Christian writer Tertullian, who lived in the second century, tells us that the heathens made use of a holy water, and ascribed to it the power not only of washing away bodily uncleanliness, but also of wiping out sin.

Among the Jews blessed water had a particular signification. They had especial laws for the use of the so-called water of aspersion. For instance, "he that toucheth the corpse of a man, and is therefore unclean seven days, shall be sprinkled with this water on the third day, and on the seventh, and so shall be cleansed." (Num. xix.) And not only such persons were to be sprinkled with this water, but also their dwellings and their furniture. "And a man that is clean shall dip hyssop in it, and shall sprinkle therewith all the tent, and all the furniture, and the men that are defiled." (Num. xix.) So important was this sprinkling that any one who was defiled "and not sprinkling with this mixture, shall profane the tabernacle of the Lord, and shall perish out of Israel, because he was not sprinkled with the water of expiation." (Num. xix. 13.)

It is evident that this expiation was not a cleansing from sin, for it can certainly not be held a sin to confer upon the dead a corporal work of mercy. Holy writ praises the good Tobias because he buried the dead. (Tob. xii. 12.) But because death is a consequence of sin, and in a measure bears with it the stain of sin, and because God would make plain to the Israelites the malice of sin, He ordained that all who came in contact with a corpse, and thus likewise with death, thus in a certain measure too became contaminated with sin stain, should be held corporally unclean. And from this uncleanliness should the Jew become cleansed by holy water.

The sacred water of heathen use, of

which mention has been made, is the foreshadow of the waters of expiation used by the Jews, and likewise a forepicture of the sacred waters which we Catholics know as holy water.

"The use of holy water comes to us, in the Catholic Church, with all that is in its favor, even from the Old Testament. It signifies now, as then, cleansing, as did the ablutions commanded in the old law, by Almighty God, down to the baptism by John in Jordan's waters. Who would gainsay that our Lord used water for this same purpose when washing the disciples' feet on the eve of His sufferings. And again, He made water a condition necessary for salvation: 'Unless a man be born again of water he cannot enter the Kingdom of Heaven.' (John iii. 5.)

"Holy water has been used in the church as it is now, through the centuries, back to the Apostles' days. It is spoken of in the 'Apostolic Constitutions.' Pope

Alexander, who died in the year 130, in his pontifical decree confirming this Apostolic tradition says: 'We bless salt and water for the people, that all who may be sprinkled therewith may be cleansed and sanctified.' The martyr St. Justin, who died in the year 163, tells us that the faithful in his time were sprinkled in their assemblies with holy water every Sunday. So too we find holy water mentioned in St. Cyprian's writings in the third century, in the works of St. Basil in the fourth, in the writings of St. Jerome in the fifth, and by St. Gregory the Great in the sixth century." (McKernon.)

Venite ad me omnes, qui laboratis, et onerati estis. Matth. 11,28.

CHAPTER II

Holy Water a Sacramental; Its Relation to the Sacraments

Holy water is one of the Sacramentals, which are things made sacred by rites of the church in the manner of Christ. In the Catholic Church we have sacraments and sacramentals. These latter differ from the sacraments. Christ our Lord gave us the sacraments. The Church, exercising the authority He gave her, instituted the sacramentals. They differ also in this: the sacraments of themselves upon worthy reception confer that particular grace which Christ attached to each of them; the sacramentals do not confer but obtain grace, as does, for instance, prayer. They who make use of them in a pious disposition have great advantages from them. They incite piety and thus cause the remission of venial sins. They likewise cause the remission of temporal punishments due to sin. They put to flight and stay the power of the devil. They obtain bodily health and other temporal benefits. These blessings follow as the effects of the prayers of the church which are used in blessing and consecrating the sacramentals. All religious rites and sacred things used in administering the sacraments are sacramentals; as for instance, the holy oils, blessed salt, holy water, the sign of the cross.

Whilst some of the sacraments are necessary for salvation, we cannot claim this for the sacramentals. Consequently, holy water is not necessary for salvation. But though it is not thus necessary it is beneficial and helpful. To ascertain this still better we will consider the effects flowing from the pious use of holy water. These effects may best be learned from the prayers pronounced by the priest in blessing the water.

CHAPTER III

Blessing of the Water

Holy water consists of a mixture of blessed salt and blessed water. The priest, as the minister of the church, first blesses salt which he afterwards puts into the water. Blessing of salt and casting of it into the water is following the example of the prophet Eliseus, who by God's command took salt and cast it into the unwholesome waters of Jericho, and made them good. "And the men of the city said to Eliseus: Behold the situation of this city is very good, as thou my Lord seest; but the waters are very bad, and the ground barren. And he said: Bring me a new vessel, and put salt into it. And when they had brought it, he went out to the spring of the waters, cast the salt into it and said: Thus saith the Lord: I have healed these waters, and there shall be no more in them death or barrenness. And the waters were healed unto this day, according to the word of Eliseus which he spoke." (4 Kings ii. 19–22.)

Calling upon God's assistance, the priest, making upon himself the sign of the cross, says: "Our help is in the name of the Lord. Who created heaven and earth." Hereupon he pronounces a prayer over the salt to free it from the curse which God pronounced upon creation as a consequence of Adam's sin. By this curse Satan gained power over creatures and he seeks thereby also to harm mankind. This power of Satan is now to be broken, so that he may no longer be able to exercise power over this salt. The priest spreads his hand over the salt and pronounces the following prayer:

"Our help is in the name of the Lord. Who hath made heaven and earth. I exorcise thee, thou creature salt, by the living God, by the true God, by the holy God, by the God who commanded thee to be cast into the water by Eliseus, the prophet, that the sterility of the water might be healed, that thou mayest become salt exorcised unto the healing of the faithful; that thou become health of soul and body to all who take thee; that every delusion and wickedness and snare of diabolical cunning and every unclean spirit may depart from the place in which thou shalt be sprinkled, when adjured by Him who is to come to judge the living and the dead and the world by fire. Amen.

"Let us pray. We humbly implore Thy boundless clemency, Almighty and everlasting God, that of Thy bounty Thou wouldst deign to bless and sanctify this creature salt, which Thou hast given for the use of mankind; let it be unto all who take it health of mind and body; that whatsoever shall be touched or sprinkled with it be freed from all manner of uncleanness, and from all assaults of spiritual wickedness. Through our Lord Jesus Christ who liveth and reigneth with Thee in the unity of the Holy Ghost for ever. Amen."

In the following prayer the blessing is pronounced over the water:

"I exorcise thee, O creature water, in the name of God the Father Almighty, and in the name of Jesus Christ His Son, our Lord; and in the power of the Holy Ghost; that Thou mayest become water exorcised for the chasing away of all the power of the enemy; that thou mayest have strength to uproot and cast out the enemy himself and his apostate angels, by the power of the same our Lord Jesus Christ, who shall come to judge the living and the dead, and the world by fire. Amen.

"Let us pray. O God, who for the salvation of mankind has founded one of Thy greatest Sacraments in the element of water, graciously give ear when we call upon Thee, and pour upon this element, prepared for divers purifications, the power of Thy blessing; let Thy creature serving in Thy Mysteries, by divine grace be effectual for casting out devils and for driving away diseases, that on whatsoever in the houses or places of the faithful this water shall be sprinkled, it may be freed from all uncleanness, and delivered from hurt. Let not the blast of pestilence nor disease remain there; let every enemy that lieth in wait depart; and if there be aught which hath ill-will to the safety and quietness of the inhabitants, let it flee away at the sprinkling of this water, that they, being healed by the invocation of Thy holy name, may be defended from all that rise up against them. Through our Lord Jesus Christ, who in unity with Thee and the Holy Ghost liveth and reigneth for ever. Amen."

The priest then mingles the salt with water in the form of a cross, saying: "Let this become a mixture of salt and water, in the name of the Father, and of the Son, and of the Holy Ghost. Amen."

"The Lord be with you. And with thy spirit. Let us pray. O God, Author of invincible might, King of unconquerable dominion, and ever a Conqueror who doest wonders, who puttest down the strength of all that rise up against Thee; who overcomest the rage of the adversary; who by Thy power doest cast down his wickedness; we, O Lord, with fear and trembling, humbly entreat and implore Thee to mercifully look upon this creature of salt and water, to graciously illumine and sanctify it with the dew of Thy favor; that wheresoever it shall be sprinkled, by the invocation of Thy holy name, all troubling of unclean spirits may be cast out, and the dread of the poisonous serpent be chased far away; and let the presence of the Holy Ghost vouchsafe to be with us, who ask Thy mercy, in every place. Through our Lord Jesus Christ who lives and reigns with Thee in unity with this same Holy Spirit for ever. Amen."

From these beautiful prayers of sanctification it is plain that we can gain graces for body and soul.

The question naturally presents itself, whence come the effects of holy water?

CHAPTER IV

The Effects of Holy Water

a. THEIR CAUSES

For the effects of holy water we are indebted principally to our divine Savior. He merited for us the graces we obtain through its usage by His bitter passion and death. Holy Church, however, who is the custodian of these precious and infinite treasures of grace merited by our Lord, has, in view of these merits, attached these effects to holy water. The power for doing this she has from Christ Himself. Hence we owe the effects of holy water primarily to Christ, and secondarily to the will and the prayers of the Church.

Concerning the effects, it is to be noted that by holy water sanctifying grace is not conferred, but actual grace is obtained, such grace for instance through which the intellect is enlightened and the will is moved to avoid evil and to do good. Corporal benefits also are obtained by holy water.

But do we wish to obtain great effects from the use of holy water, then must we be correspondingly well prepared. To be thus prepared we must above all be in the state of grace and have firm faith in and submission to Christ and His holy Church. By this it must not be understood that to one even thus disposed all the effects attached to the use of holy water will be granted, but we know that whosoever takes holy water in the proper disposition, graces will be accorded. How many graces or favors one obtains cannot be determined. Nor will one invariably obtain the good or the grace that he seeks to obtain through holy water however well he may be prepared. For instance, holy water is taken to relieve the subject from sickness. He takes it with firm faith and great confidence. Will he be cured without fail? No. On the contrary, however, he will invariably obtain some other grace which is equally as important to him, or more so.

But why does holy water not infallibly bring the desired effect, even though used with a proper disposition?

The Catechism teaches that the sacramentals, consequently holy water, operate principally by means of the Church's intercession. The Church is the bride of the Divine Savior, and hence her prayers are always pleasing to God. When the Church prays, the divine bridegroom prays with her, and for this reason her prayer is powerful with God. Thus it may happen that a lukewarm Christian may derive great benefit from the use of holy water. The reason for this is that God does not look so much upon the unworthiness of mankind, but rather looks upon the prayer of the Church, so pleasing to Him. Especially though will the loyal children of the Church, who seek to coordinate their ideas to those of the Divine Savior and of the Church, participate in the blissful effects of holy water.

Thus far the effects of holy water have been considered in a general way; they shall now be treated of in detail.

These are, as previously stated, of a twofold nature: the effects of grace for the body and the effects of grace for the soul. Words used in the first prayer which the Church pronounces in blessing the salt are "that thou be to all who take thee, salvation of soul and body," and in the second prayer, "let it be to all who take it, health of mind and body." Inasmuch as harmful influences, and sometimes sickness, originate largely with the devil, the prayer of the Church in the blessing of the water directs herself principally against the evil spirit, and consequently holy water is in an especial manner a means of protection against this evil spirit.

b. EFFECTS FOR THE WELFARE OF THE BODY

As we learn from these same prayers of the Church, holy water is a special remedy against ills of the body. This effect is contained in the second prayer pronounced over the water. Therein the Church thus addresses herself to God: "Graciously give ear when we call upon Thee, and pour upon this element . . . the power of Thy blessing; let Thy creature . . . by Divine grace be effectual for driving away diseases, that on whatsoever in the houses or places of the faithful this water shall be sprinkled, it be freed from all uncleanness, and be delivered from hurt."

From these words it is plain that holy

water is not only a means to drive away sickness, but is likewise a protection against sickness.

But Holy Church in her prayer for the bodily welfare of her children shows still more foresight. She knows well that not only corporal sufferings, but misfortune in temporal possessions as well, are painful to mankind. Holy Church consequently offers a means of protection against such mishaps, when she implores in the second prayer over the water, "let not the blast of pestilence nor disease remain" where this water is sprinkled. All harmful influence of the elements, and the powers of the enemy, the Church wishes to keep from mankind, and hence she prays: "and if there be aught which hath ill will to the safety and quietness of the inhabitants, let it flee away at the sprinkling of this water."

Thus holy water advances the bodily welfare of the faithful. A brief narrative will show us that it also achieves the advancement of the soul's welfare.

C. EFFECTS FOR THE GOOD OF THE SOUL

As the soul is far superior to the body, so too are the spiritual effects of holy water superior to the effects corporal. The prayers used in the blessing do not specify these spiritual effects, they speak only in general of the advancement of our soul's salvation through this holy water. For example, in the prayers which are said over the salt the words occur, "be to all who take thee salvation of soul and body," and "health of mind and body." In like manner the spiritual effect is expressed only in a general way in the concluding prayer when the Church directs her petition to God that He may illumine and sanctify the salt and the water, "that wheresoever it shall be sprinkled, by the invocation of Thy holy name all troubling of unclean spirits may be cast out, and the dread of the poisonous serpent be chased far away; and let the presence of the Holy Ghost vouchsafe to be with us, who ask thy mercy, in every place."

In these words the petition is that holy water may shield us against the influence of the evil one, — hence the purifying effect — and secure for us assistance in the grace of the Holy Ghost, wherein is expressed the sanctifying effect.

That holy water possesses this purifying and sanctifying effect is indicated in the following prayer used by the Church in its distribution: "Thou shalt sprinkle me, O Lord, with hyssop, and I shall be cleansed: Thou shalt wash me, and I shall be made whiter than snow . . . and all unto whom that water came were saved." These words clearly point to a purifying and sanctifying effect of holy water. We may not, however, conclude from this that any purifying from mortal sin takes place, because none of the sacramentals cleanses from such sin; but we are correct in assuming a purifying from venial sin and from temporal punishments due to sin.

Doctors of the Church agree that holy water causes the remission of venial sin and of temporal punishment due to sin. I quote St. Thomas Aquinas: "By the sprinkling of holy water the debt of venial sin is wiped out; but not always, however, are all temporal punishments relinquished; this takes place in proportion to the disposition of the person using it, depending upon the less or greater degree of ardor in the love for God on the part of the person using it." Again the same holy Doctor says that "the sprinkling of holy water brings about the remission of venial sin in the measure of which it excites to contrition." In accord with the advice of St. Alphonsus one should strive when using holy water to rise to contrition, that it may prove its purifying effects.

Holy water possesses not only the power of cleansing us from venial sin and temporal punishments, but also helps us to overcome the temptations of the devil. To bring about this effect holy Church asks in the first prayer pronounced over the salt that Almighty God may effect that it serve for the preservation of the people, that "every delusion and wickedness of the devil, and all unclean spirits, fly and depart." Still more. In the second prayer over the salt, it shall even shield us against all assaults of spiritual wickedness; hence thus to protect us against temptation, that the devil may have even less power to tempt us.

Holy water also has sanctifying effects. These consist in the actual graces which may be obtained. These are illumining the intellect, and inspirations of the Holy Ghost which aid the faithful to loyally perform the duties of their state of life, to pray devoutly, to hear a sermon with profit, and especially to assist with recollection and devotion at the Holy Sacrifice of Mass, and thus richly participate in its precious treasures. An illumination, for instance, may be when one learns to understand, better than he has known, to comprehend his faults, and particularly his prevailing sin. An inspiration, however, is when an inward voice admonishes him to finally resolve to avoid the occasion of sin, to give up a sinful acquaintance, to shun bad associations, or dangerous occasions, with greater determination, and to seek after, with a special devotion and earnestness, that virtue which is in opposition to his prevailing vice. These are effects of the actual graces, effects which holy water can bring about. I do not maintain that the above-named or similar effects of grace must necessarily be attributed to the use of holy water, because we cannot know what and how much it has effected in us. But we do know that it can produce these effects, and we may without doubt have occasion to attribute much of our knowledge and inspiration to the use of holy water.

CHAPTER V

The Application of Holy Water by the Church

As holy water can accomplish so many sided effects for body and soul, it is easily understood why the Church should adapt its use in many ways in her divine service, and likewise recommend its pious usage to the faithful. Its most solemn use by the Church is in the "Asperges," in sprinkling the faithful, previous to the principal service of Sundays.

As the Lord's Prayer is denoted the "Our Father" because it begins with these words, so is the giving of holy water before the beginning of Sunday service styled "Asperges," because the prayer which the priest offers in distributing holy water begins with the words "Asperges." The hymn "Asperges me Domine hyssopo et mundabor, lavabis me, et super nivem dealbabor," reads in English, "Thou shalt sprinkle me, O Lord, with hyssop, and I shall be cleansed: Thou shalt wash me, and I shall be made whiter than snow."

According to the prescribed rule of the Church, holy water shall be given on Sunday only, and then just preceding the principal morning service. The priest to officiate at this service, first sprinkles himself, then the altar, then the faithful. The altar is a symbol of Christ, but the priest is the mediator between Christ and the people. By this sprinkling of the altar and the people, expression is given to the idea that Christ and the faithful form a unit, that the people are members of the mystic body of Christ. So, then, the altar is the place where the Holy Sacrifice of the Mass, the unbloody offering of the

New Testament, is presented, and is therefore a place whence flow many graces for the faithful. Precisely this fulness of grace which the faithful receive is plainly typified because the priest goes from the altar, out among the people, to sprinkle them. But because the priest, before beginning Holy Mass, sprinkles himself, the altar, and the faithful, there is therefore something else quite special to be attained. It is this: The priest, the altar, the faithful, shall become, as much as can be, clean and holy, for the worthy celebration of Holy Mass. No one indeed can say that he is too pure to offer, or to assist at, this Holy Sacrifice. And if in the Old Testament they who according to the law were unclean must first be purified by sprinkling of the water of expiation, that they might become worthy to assist at the sacrificial acts, how much the more does the infinite sanctity of the sacrifice of the New Testament demand that all who assist thereat shall in so far as is possible become purified.

During the Easter season, instead of the "Asperges," the "Vidi Aquam" is intoned. "Vidi aquam egredientem de templo a latere dextero, alleluia: et omnes, ad quos pervenit aqua ista, salvi facti sunt et dicent, alleluia, alleluia." Given in English: "I saw water flowing from the right side of the temple, Alleluia; and all to whom that water came were saved, and they shall say, Alleluia, alleluia." The "Vidi Aquam" was chanted in the first centuries of the Christian era, but from emotions different from those of to-day. In those days it was sung by the newly baptized, who had received baptism on Holy Saturday. These daily walked in procession at Vesper tide during the Easter week, to the baptismal font, and chanted, besides other anthems, the "Vidi Aquam." As the Church intones this hymnal at Easter time she desires to direct our mind to the water of holy baptism, and likewise to that water which flowed from the opened side of the Divine Redeemer, and also to the rich source of grace, and from which at Easter time all Christendom is bedewed with spiritual renewal, expiation, and sanctification. The Alleluias of this Canticle bring expression to the joy over the resurrection of the divine Savior, and find an echo in the soul of every believing Christian; for through holy baptism we, too, have spiritually risen with Christ.

As previously remarked, the Asperges preceding the principal Sunday service is the solemn ceremony through which holy water finds its application. In a less solemn manner the Asperges is applied on pastoral visits. When the priest enters the room of the sick, he sprinkles the sick, and likewise the room, with holy water, meanwhile reciting the Asperges. By this sprinkling shall be banished any possible evil influence from the sick and from the dwelling.

The Church furthermore uses holy water in blessings and dedications, and indeed it is used in most of these.

When, for example, the priest offers the blessing over the sick, he sprinkles him with holy water. When, as is the custom in some localities, wine is blessed on the feast of St. John the Evangelist, or bread on the feast of St. Agatha, or when incense is blest on Epiphany, or the ashes on Ash Wednesday, or palms on Palm Sunday, all these objects to be blest are sprinkled with holy water. In like manner holy water forms an important factor in the blessing of a house, a bridge, a railroad, or a telegraph system.

Thus is holy water used in most blessings and dedications. In many of these it has a higher meaning than at first glance would appear. And this great significance consists in this, that by the sprinkling of holy water the object to be blessed receives the same power that rests in the holy water. These effects can be imparted by the priest or by any believer. If the priest imparts them he does so in asking from God, in the name of the Church, those particular effects which he hopes for in the object blest. If the faithful perform the ceremony, then the effects of holy water are merely transferred to the receiving object. The objects here considered are either food or drink, medicines or like articles.

The Church uses holy water in funeral ceremonies.

As every Catholic Christian knows from his catechism, the Church militant, the Church suffering, and the Church triumphant constitute the Communion of Saints, a mystical body of which Christ is the head. The Church militant can aid the Church suffering by her intercession. This intercessory prayer may be the offering of the Holy Sacrifice of Mass, the application of indulgences, good works, or prayers, — offered for the souls in purgatory. When the Church sprinkles holy water in funeral ceremonies, her prayerful hope and wish is symbolized, that the soul of the departed may be expiated and sanctified for the great day of judgment. To make this hope effective the Church joins the sprinkling with a prayer. When the priest receives the corpse, having sprinkled the coffin with holy water, he recites Ps. cxxix. In this psalm the abiding hope is expressed that the deceased may find mercy with God, and at its conclusion the petition is added, "Eternal rest grant unto him, O Lord, and let perpetual light shine upon him." And whilst the priest three times sprinkles the body when lowered into the grave, he prays, "May the soul be refreshed in the Heavenly Kingdom by the Almighty God, the Father, the Son, and the Holy Ghost. Amen." And how impressive the prayer of the Church, which while at the coffin she sends to heaven in the name of the deceased, before sprinkling the holy water: "Deliver me, O Lord, from eternal death in that awful day: when the heavens and the earth shall be shaken: when Thou shalt come to judge the world by fire." And whilst the priest sprinkles the holy water he recites the "Our Father."

As the dew refreshes the flowers that have been exposed to the rays of the sun, so holy water, the heavenly dew, conjoined with prayer, refreshes the souls in purgatory and lessens their sufferings. Dives, suffering in hell, asked in vain that Abraham but dip a finger into water and cool his parching tongue. His wish was not granted. Hell is barred by the justice of God so that no mercy can enter there. In purgatory, however, mercy still has an entrance. Holy Church, our Mother, dips her blessing hand into the sanctified water to soothe the burning pains of the suffering souls.

The Church applies holy water in funeral ceremonies not only to aid the soul of the departed, but likewise for the sake of the lifeless body. The blessed water shall effect it unto sanctification. This body was a temple of the Holy Ghost, the bearer of an immortal soul, which will be again united on the last day. The Church consequently sanctifies the corruptible corpse that it may be the more worthy to become an incorruptible body unto resurrection, to be forever the dwelling place of the soul. For the same reason the corpse of a child is sprinkled with holy water, and likewise also is the grave blessed. Thus is enhanced the dignity of the corpse that is bedded to rest in a home of earth. At the same time this occurs, too, to keep from the grave any influence of Satan.

CHAPTER VI

Application of Holy Water by the Faithful

We have studied how the Church makes use of holy water. But it is her earnest wish that the faithful likewise make pious and fervent use of this means of grace. She therefore on every Sunday, excepting Easter and Pentecost Sundays, in those churches where baptismal water was blessed on the previous day, blesses water and keeps it in a place and vessel especially adapted for this purpose. From this the faithful can, and should, carry it to their homes. In keeping with this the Roman Ritual admonishes the faithful to take of the blessed water with them, and to sprinkle the sick, the homes, and the fields. And, too, they should keep it in their apartments, and frequently during the day sprinkle themselves with it.

In the church edifice the faithful are offered an opportunity to participate in the sanctifying effects of holy water, for in every church there is at least one holy water vase attached, that the people upon entering and leaving the building may take holy water.

Upon entering the church holy water should awaken a contrite disposition in the faithful, that they may appear in God's presence with a pure heart. And then shall the mind be purified of worldly thoughts which so greatly disturb devotion and recollection in prayer. The faithful should herein follow the example of St. Stephen, the third Abbot of Citeaux, whose biographers relate that upon entering the church he was wont to close the door after him and say—"You thoughts of worldly affairs remain outside, and await my return. I have no use of you now, as I have an important task to perform. My time is now entirely taken up with God." These thoughts should likewise fill the hearts of the faithful when entering the church they take holy water.

Upon leaving the church, they should join with the sprinkling of holy water a prayer to God that He would guard the good thoughts and strengthen the good resolutions formed during divine services.

Thus Holy Church plainly shows her endeavor to gain for the faithful the beneficial effects of holy water, who on their part should enter into this spirit of Mother Church, and take holy water not only in the house of worship but should often use it in their dwellings, and consequently it should also be found in every Catholic home. With every family there should be a well-filled holy water vase and every member of the family should enjoy the opportunity it affords. It is a beautiful and praiseworthy custom to take holy water when rising in the morning and when retiring at night.

When a new day dawns, who will say what it may bring with it? Who can foretell the dangers that may await the life of the body, or the more precious life of the soul! Though the Christian, even if he be in the state of sanctifying grace, has much to lose, it is certainly a measure of prudence to use every means at his disposal to guard against any loss of this precious treasure.

We have no doubt sufficiently indicated that holy water is precisely a special safeguard against all dangers. What! If with a drop of holy water one makes the sign of the cross upon his forehead, he can banish the roaring lion, the devilish enemy, is it not worth while in time of temptation to use holy water? And again: If the believing Christian considers what dangers he may encounter when entering the mining shaft, or ascending to the burning oven, serving at the machines in the great factories, traveling on railways or steamships,—in short there are so many dangers, even for the laborer, for the husbandman on the farm, that he ought be glad, every morning, to make use of holy water that he may share in the blessings and prayers of Holy Church.

Many dangers likewise threaten the children, dangers to body and soul. The child is inexperienced and does not dream of danger. Ofttimes the parents are careless, or haven't the time or opportunity to sufficiently guard their children. And how numerous too are the dangers for the soul of the child. It becomes almost impossible for the parents alone to ward these off entirely from their children. Unfortunately there are too many of the enemy who seek to sow the seed of wrong into the heart of the innocent child. What better can parents do who are concerned about the welfare of their children than to recommend them to God's protection and to the care of their guardian angel, to which act we would direct especial attention, — what better can they do than to give them the holy water, and gradually lead them on to its use, that by this means they share in the prayers of the Church, and thus safely place them against the influences of the demon and the manifold dangers to body and soul?

Not only in broad daylight, but even in darkness, is mankind threatened with dangers. Man may rest, but the devil never. At night, and particularly at night, he plans ruin to the soul of man. When the pious Christian is about to lay himself to rest, and with holy water marks his forehead, his lips and his heart, he well may earnestly plead with God to shield him against the delusions of the devil. For this indeed does the Church pray in her blessings that "every delusion and wickedness of the devil depart" by virtue of holy water. Consequently, one will take holy water at eventide to cleanse the soul from the venial sins of the passing day, as also to rest secure for the night against the onslaughts of the evil spirit.

It is well also to suggest that holy water is a wholesome remedy for the sick. Let them who nurse the sick be concerned that they have opportunity to use holy water, nor let the sick neglect often to sprinkle themselves with it, being mindful of the prayers of the Church, that holy water may possess the power of driving away sickness. Convinced of this, the invalid cannot too often take advantage of the opportunity given. He may likewise sprinkle in the manner of a cross the medicinal remedies to be used. When the patient suffers, and is in misery from pain, let him use it with confidence and prayer. When the death struggle approaches and the demon redoubles his efforts, then especially should the patient be frequently sprinkled with the sanctified water, mindful that Holy Church implores in her prayers and blessings against the onslaughts of the devil. The Church especially advises that holy water should be carried to the home in order to sprinkle the sick.

Not alone man, but whatever stands in relation to him, shall by the use of holy water be protected against the power of the destroying angel of wickedness. It is therefore the desire of Holy Church that the faithful sprinkle holy water in their houses, and upon their fields, to keep away damaging influences, and to intercede for the fruitfulness of their acres. For these effects does the Church in her blessings thus implore: "that on whatsoever in the houses or in the places of the faithful this water shall be sprinkled, it may be freed from all uncleanness, and delivered from hurt. Let not the blast of pestilence nor disease remain there; and if there be aught which hath ill-will to the safety and quiet of the inhabitants, let it flee away at the sprinkling of this water."

From what has been said it is easy to observe how manifold are the effects of holy water. We cannot at once grasp all these effects nor have them in view at the moment of using it. We should, however, aim to use it with devotion and confidence, then we may confidently hope that God will have us share in precisely those effects that will be most beneficial for our bodily and spiritual welfare, even though at the time we had no thought of these.

As Mother Church gives holy water to her deceased members, so is it her wish that the faithful should give it to their departed. Therefore it is a genuine Catholic custom, for the faithful, as is the case in many places when assisting at the "death watch," to sprinkle the corpse with holy water and also to perform the same pious act when visiting "God's Acre," to sprinkle the grave with holy water. Nor should there be omission at the same time to pray for the suffering souls, which is in accord with the examples of Holy Church, for instance, "Eternal rest grant unto them, O Lord, and let perpetual light shine upon them. May they rest in peace. Amen."* Thus holy water becomes a sort of heavenly dew that refreshes the souls in purgatory and soothes their sufferings.

---

* This short prayer commends itself particularly because it is enriched with an indulgence of 200 days, applicable to the souls in purgatory. (Leo. xiii., 1880.)

We adduce other prayers to which an indulgence is attached, that may be gained as often every day as desirable, if recited with piety and contrition, and is applicable to the souls in purgatory.

"Sweet heart of Jesus, grant that I may love thee more and more. (300 days. Pius ix., 26th Nov., 1876.)

"Sweet heart of Mary, be my Salvation. (300 days. Pius ix., 30th Sept., 1852.)

"Jesus, Mary, Joseph, I give you my heart and my soul. Jesus, Mary, Joseph, assist me in my last agony.

Herewith this treatise on holy water is brought to a close. We give, however, a brief reply to some questions which may elucidate what has been said, and will solve some possible doubts.

Jesus, Mary, Joseph, may my soul depart in peace with you." (300 days. Pius vii., 28th April, 1807.)

"My Jesus, mercy." (100 days. Pius ix., 24th Sept., 1846.)

"Sweetest Jesus, be not my judge, but my Redeemer." (50 days. Pius ix., Aug. 11, 1851.)

"Jesus my God, I love Thee above all else." (50 days. Pius ix., May 7, 1854.)

"Eternal Father, I offer the precious blood of Jesus Christ in expiation of my sins and for the wants of the Church." (100 days. Pius vii., 22d Sept., 1817.)

In pious invocation of the name of "Jesus." (25 days. Clement xiii., 5th Sept., 1759.)

"Praised be Jesus Christ." — Answer: "For ever, Amen." Or, "Amen." (50 days, if pronounced with first part, and answered. Clement xiii., 5th Sept., 1759.)

"In the name of the Father, and of the Son, and of the Holy Ghost (Amen)." (50 days, as often as the sign of the cross is made while expressing the invocation. Pius ix., 28th July, 1863. — 100 days as often as using holy water and making the sign of the cross. Pius. ix., 23d March, 1866.)

(*a*) How ancient is the use of holy water in the Catholic Church?

As most all doctrines and ordinances of the Catholic Church have been subjected to antagonism and scorn, so has holy water been the subject of attack upon the Church. It has been charged that the Church brought about the use of holy water in the later centuries. Against these attacks be it remarked: The prayers and ceremonies by which water is blest, are, as may readily be perceived, so serious and elevated, their significance so great, that only a malicious disposition would trifle with such means of grace. As concerns the use of holy water, it is undoubtedly very ancient. In a writing bearing the title "Apostolic Constitutions," composed at the very latest in the year 400, there is mention of a blessed water effective for the protection of health, the healing of the sick, the keeping away of demons and all that is evil, the same as the holy water of the present day. Without any doubt, however, the use of such a sacramental in the Church is still more ancient. Furthermore, the prayers which the priest uses at present in blessing water, which have been quoted, are found in our exact wording in a book written by Pope St. Gregory the Great (who died in 604).

But what about the objection that holy water is an innovation by the Church? We have already stated that holy water is a sacramental, and that the sacramentals were not ordained by Christ, but by the Catholic Church through the authority of Christ. Christ said to the Supreme Head of the Church, "Amen I say to you, Whatsoever you shall bind upon earth shall be bound also in heaven; and whatsoever you shall loose upon earth shall be loosed also in heaven." The Church consequently could ordain the use of holy water at any time in her pleasure, as she could also discontinue it if she deemed it advisable or necessary. Holy Church, therefore, merely exercised her prerogative or right in establishing the use of holy water.

(*b*) Another question that arises here concerns especially the Asperges before the principal Sunday service. When the holy water is distributed it is quite probable that many of the faithful are not reached by it. These to some extent are therefore of the opinion that they do not share in its distribution. This fear is without foundation. For even if they are not reached by it, they can nevertheless participate in its effects, if they are desirous of participation, and manifest this desire by some outward sign; for instance, by rising, by bowing the head, or making upon themselves the sign of the cross.

In like manner it is not necessary, in the blessing of the palms on Palm Sunday, or the blessing of herbs on the feast of the Assumption of the Blessed Virgin, that each palm or each herb be reached or touched by the holy water, but it is sufficient that the priest conducting the ceremony have the intention to bless the palms or objects placed before him, which is, of course, always the case.

(*c*) Another instance which sometimes receives too little attention is the cleanliness of the holy water vases. It is a matter easy of oversight to fail in purifying them before renewing the supply of newly blest water. It may happen that for weeks and months one keeps adding without thinking of cleansing the vase of the sediments which are apt to gather. To this circumstance may in a measure be attributed the frequent attacks to which holy water is exposed in latter years. It is sometimes charged that these vases are breeding places for bacilli. Want of cleanliness in this respect, which is the case, sad be it to remark, in many places, has given occasion for the attack. Therefore, regard should be had for the cleanliness of the vases, and for the use of pure, clean water; then there can be no fear of contagion. When it is desirable to clean the vase, what shall be done with the residue? It may be poured into the garden or upon the meadow or upon any appropriate spot where it will not be subjected to disrespect.

(*d*) Another question. If the holy water at hand might not be sufficient for the occasion, may water that is not blessed be added? Yes. But care must be taken not to add as great a quantity as there is of holy water.

Conclusion

We have briefly shown the significancy of holy water which it possesses in the sanctifying order. The believing Christian knows well that it is not sufficient merely to take or use the holy water to make secure of its effects, but that it is necessary to avoid sin, and the occasions of sin, to keep God's commands, to make use of the means of grace, and to lead a pious Christian life. From the above deductions it is plain that holy water is likewise to be appreciated as an aid to further the temporal and spiritual welfare of man. Hence there should not be any further need of encouragement for the earnest Christian to make frequent use of it; he is encouraged to do so by the thought that our Divine Savior, by the spilling of His precious blood, has merited the graces of which through this blessed water we may become participants. He is also encouraged by the fact that our Holy Mother, the Church, who is so earnestly desirous of the welfare of her children, wishes that we persistently use it. Finally he is encouraged to do this by the consideration of the effects of holy water for both body and soul. Could it be possible that an earnest Catholic would close his ears to this threefold incentive?

Surely not. Rather would his debt of love and gratitude to the Divine Savior and to the Church, as well as his anxiety for his own corporal and spiritual welfare, be an incentive to him, cheerfully, often, and with confidence and devotion, to make use of holy water.

Let us follow the admonition of the Holy Ghost: "Haurietis aquas in gaudio de fontibus salvatoris—You shall draw water with joy out of the Savior's fountains." (Is. xii. 3.)

CONTENTS